FINISHING LINE PRESS

www.finishinglinepress.com

heliophobia

poems by

Saba Syed Razvi

Finishing Line Press
Georgetown, Kentucky

heliophobia

Publisher: Leah Maines

Editor: Christen Kincaid

Cover Art: "The Dervish Arranged for Them to Be Together in the Graveyard",
Illustration for The Arabian Nights, Artist: Kay Rasmus Nielsen (March 12,
1886—June 21, 1957), Image in Public Domain.

Author Photo: Saba Syed Razvi

Cover Design: Elizabeth Maines McCleavy

Printed in the USA on acid-free paper.
Order online: www.finishinglinepress.com
          also available on amazon.com

Author inquiries and mail orders:
Finishing Line Press
P. O. Box 1626
Georgetown, Kentucky 40324
U. S. A.

Table of Contents

The Moon can be an earth complete with mountains and valleys, and the earth can be a star. An ordinary celestial body, one of thousands. Take another look. Does the dark part of the moon look completely dark to you?

—*Life of Galileo.* Bertolt Brecht.

i.

Higher
than the dark top of the sky
higher
in a mad opening
a trail of light
is the halo of death.

—Bataille, *Oresteia*

Nereid Speaking

Rising, this is. From beneath
the current—I am
stretched too thin, high
and pushed higher, carrying
in offering this disk of pearl
on my crest. I will break—
a thousand parts, globe and
opalescent far brighter than this
slice of moon. These rocks
to hold me
in shivering pools: barriers
against the smooth expanse of
blue—
dry over slick, the same
shade of calming. Here
I take the reflection
                    apart,
here, the rigid crux of cliff
and breaking surf. In this
sea foam: not birth, but where
I come to die. Command me,
will you, Oread? Command me
and I will come, fall at your eroding
feet, forward, breaking, from you.

Lorca at the Edge of the Sea

These waves falling endlessly
on the unsteady sand, see them,
folding over on their haunches
prostrate—they are
naiads, rising from the heavy
beds of clay to surrender you
to the rough, sifting dunes.
This sound
is their lament, a choir of breaking.
Listen, listen for the lull of it, they
changing, cannot bear
the unchanging of your body there.
See, see how they have brought
the unsunken husk of you, so full
of their own breath, back
to the surface. And yet
you are lying still on the wet sand,
slipping away around you and leaving
a bed. See how they move
your body against themselves, wavering
like the sound of regret, your body
like a ripple left on the sand.
Your legs like the cleaving,
splitting, fusing of a mermaid's fin and in
this coupling,
they are desperate
to birth you in this foam. But you are not
like Aphrodite, not like anyone, but
perhaps Echo - because in this unstitching
you are coming apart and coming
back and you are everywhere around this
scene but where your body
lies, brought like a gift from the sea.
Your body, lost but for them
not bullet-ridden, but studded
with pearls, sprouting moons, shimmering
the holes in your skin.

First Night in the New House

The moon hung low overhead:
not a paper lantern,
but an amber orb.
Bare back to bare back,
seated on the serrated incline
of rooftop,
looking up at it, we
tried to guess what insects might be
trapped inside that sticky sudden drop:
dragonflies and blue morphos,
caterpillars with—No
need for clouds
to swell and drift overhead
in shapes so bold when—
we had
the stark privacy of moon.
Our words spilled unheard off the edge:
small seeds
settling into rough, sprouting grass.
I reached back and held your hands
in mine,
never wanting to leave this
Siamese dream—my skull against yours.

Before Dawn

You cannot be real; blinking like that,
your irises not yet frozen.

Imprinted framework of pins & wire—
weight dug into a fishing net—now
a grid pressed over your bare scalp.

Not even an eyelash stray left
on your flesh, paling in the blue
light of dead stars.

                    You might well
have been beneath the tide a week,
become so like a ripple.

Elemental

Women in ancient Rome & in Pompeii
used obsidian for mirrors.

What they saw as self was shadow.

When quickersilver took the place of
slow earth's core, color glared.

Cold mimicry.

Reflections—glossy, supernatural.

In the purpled hue of volcanic glass—
the high ridge of cheekbone: sharp as a
knife edge, the bow of lip: ripened like
red fruit.

No more luminous throat, a sinistered
threat of smile.

A face instead, ordinaried as minah
birds, repeating.

Cicatrix

1. *Spiderdust*—Bel Canto

On the porous ground, fissures: filled
and spreading veins of stilled tar.
The streetlight glow shimmered, fogged.

This: a road caught in a pocket.
Of time. We: swallowed
by a starless night, a sky
as ripe as purple plumflesh.

You: luminous as a full moon
hanging at the base of sky.

2. *Dawning of the Iconoclast*—Dead Can Dance

The asphalt shouldn't have glistened
under that moonless sky—like pebbles
rippling water—when you guided my feet,
teaching me how to tango in a half-filled parking lot.

My feet—caught up
in the moving of your hands—
so fluid I could feel them slipping
too many ways.

You said I needed more hunger
in my steps, mapped out a living
connect-the-dots. Under my skin,
Pompeii stilling in an orange day.

Later, in the silver-tuned dawn,
between cruel layers
of wrinkling silk, you showed me
what hunger was.

Then—no more warmth left
in me—no red poppies opening petals to the sun.

3. *The Rapture*—Mankind is Obsolete

Sometimes the blue sky is as frozen as faith, like damselflies
                        disappointing;
St. Theresa's cold wings of ruby bone are bleached tephra
                        under the green sea.

Mother always dreaming the Rapture:

Once, flame was never *Thera* upon steps of ice,
                        the warmth of melancholy eyelids
                        that two must justify,
then singing *noli mi tangere*, after.

Not an Apple, Only Blossoms

Sudden
monochromatic shift of cloud
& under shade of canopied sky,

We listen
to the silence beyond thunder,

searching for the breath
of hidden stars
in the stripe of lightning overhead,

ancient
godwrath & secret knowledge—distilled.

The fog's descent, imperceptible,
colors the bougainvillea & magenta
glows lava-bright against green leaf, thorn.

Not sated by a rumble, we seek
fat, slipping drops of dew, pebble sharp.

Here time is reborn in the moment of fall,
when beauty is in the simple burning
ember of blossom, too full of molten sun

to leave behind. This dark
is
the antithesis of drought.

Cacophony of Bells: the Origin of Disquiet
for Fernando Pessoa

Fernando, the self you see reflected
in the liquor in your glass is not
your self. He follows you, though,
commenting on the silences you resume.

Can you blame him if he emerges
sometimes, holding your hand while you
hold the pen. Lover of ink, he is
in love with your blood.

What he doesn't see when he looks
back at you is like the sound of breaking
glass, sliver of bells crackling
between your teeth.

He will consume you, Fernando: do not
look at him.

Lullaby for Goya

In bed, I place a slip of jade beneath
the eyelids
to dull the ample edge of dreaming.
When morning falls in crisp blades
the images will fade sooner,
cut with just enough razored disc.
Otherwise, the waves would fall
in endless ripples, seams
along my skin all day, no rock
to break the rest.
And dayburnt hours are too harsh
for the slick oil of ambergris, sand.
Is it only after glass is broken
that it shimmers just so,
turning rainbows in its profiles?
And maybe your paintings of dark
on dark, too, are enough to keep
the lonely sound of hope at bay.
No, not waves! That is rain
in sheets, gliding down the brick façade
of my house, windows shivering
in lightning.
When I step outside the door, the road
will pool at my feet,
a thousand eyeless beads of water
bursting in unison.
Goya, will the sad lady guard you,
keep the sharp
winds from your tearless irises?
No harvest moon could hide behind
these tides of cumulonimbus, spilling
into evening
It is no wonder that your bristles speak
the sound of black: is it
the simplicity of truth we must deny?

The Cost of Forgiving

She watches the rippling under-tide
of river, deluge of sepiatoned
photographs, smelted into ash.

In the distance, framed by
sagging branches,
heavy drooping leaves:
two pale swans—& *doesn't*
the male always protect the
female?—overheard.

She walks closer, hand dipping
down to lift up mudwater
to blank lips.

Deep under the weight of tide, she
imagines bright, blind albino-fish
& seaweed too neon for coral reefs,
the discarded half of her
heart, there—minor husks & chambers
for the salty eggs of eels.

ii.

While the eyes of his head may sleep,
His heart will open hundreds of eyes.

—Rumi

Abida

She sits in the dawn silence—
house pulsing with dreams
& *muezzin* echoes of a faith
deeper than sleep—
fingers holding prayer beads,

counting each worry
& pushing it away
with a small *tick*
to clash into the others
on the strand of her *tasbeeh.*

Her prayer rug secure beneath her—
threadbare reds & blues
where knees & forehead have
ground faith deep
into *terra firma.*

A flame to burn down heaven,
& a sea to quench hell
& like Rabia
she sits before God,
offers her love for itself alone.

Later, there will be coffee, tea,
to be made,
sugar spoons & aspartame,
too many kinds of cracked
& cooking eggs, a rush of hands.

The sound of crumpling paper
sacks, screen doors slamming
against *Thanks,*
echoed in the scattered, unrinsed
mugs & shells.

And every 4am,

her threadbare rectangle like solid stone
waits, the beads ticking
a loop of steady gratitude.
Everywhere—peace.

Eve, Eve and Adam...Nowhere

In parts of the Mediterranean, it was not an apple
that Eve plucked from a high branch, but a fig.
In others they say pomegranate—who
defines the size of desire, the shapes of lust?

A rush of skins on skin: plucking this fruit
is leaving herself on the vines.

It is heated work to harvest figs; I spent today weaving
through three trees;
branches newly nudged aside for honey-yellowed bulbs
snap back into old places, unfurling, slap at my face.

The brightest ones soften—
already too fermented to eat.

Beneath the widest, peach-skinned grey-green leaves,
the ripest curves of bulbs shift into sight:
firm enough to grasp, pink
blush spreading from their tips, outward, into maroon.

You must twist them slowly free of their branches
until they loosen,
spilling beads of sticky, white milk
from their broken stems.

These are the ones worth rummaging for
through high, thickening branches, spiraling upward.

I brought in a basketful, rinsing off the sticky resin
in icewater
and lifting them by the handful back into dry towel.

Keep them too close and they sour quickly, unbreathing.
No pear could ever come this close to an offering.

From the Hours of Forgiveness

Red henna
for the soles of my dancing feet,
so that my footfalls can letter
the name of my own Devdas—
I have none.

Powdered *sindoor*
become red steps racing sari ribbon
to the barred gate—
I have none.

Neither am I scarred moon
nor broken star—I am
not loved so much.

What then can drown in a bottle,
a dream,
another and another breath?

When all ties fall like loosened pearls
one throb of heartbeat lives the whole
love of a lifetime in a single moment's pain.

The sound of railways moving towards
the ends of breath, and in the leaves
are the words that mean regret.

Double Edge of Scimitar

Trim your beard
a little bit shorter this time,
haaji, so your wife doesn't
smell the other woman,
still young enough to
water like a peach,
still innocent enough to think
your attentions
will lead her ascent to heavens
beyond your *hafiz* flesh.
And don't forget to shower
before you step
onto the newly-swept floor,
past the table laid out
with your wife's delicate
touch spread banquet-wide
and festive
because she knows it
isn't her you're gracing these nights,
you quick as the binding needle,
swift as the unbinding knife,
her unstitched
warmth too familiar and still
not tight enough to hold
away the clenching of a fist.
Remember, she'll lie
still as a floorboard, for you,
all the dusty creaks you expect,
but, no, don't
stay long or she will notice
other splinters, hardened
in your tauter muscles.
Better to leave her
unrewarded, contemplating her errors,
the barren hollow inside the waist,
how much more compliant she should be.

Before The Wedding Party

Textured velvet *ghararra,* skirt heavy and veil heavier,
filled crimson with gold and the intricacies of needled

fingers into patterns that catch and dispel the light
into so many glares. It is easy to sit still, head

down under a *ghoongat* veil in modest pose, when secrets
hang like sharp garlands, stone-laden at the neck,

red lips frowning at once willful knees now folded like hands
too folded on them. It befits a bride to wring her nervous

fingers, let go a show of scalding tears in anticipation.

But there's a fine unseen line, slit-skin slender, dividing
modesty from shame. Old customs die too

                              slowly, survive the young
opening angles of hips and hands, to face the limbs' deceits.

What answer then when with *henna*-ed hands so much red
undress sheds like a chameleon's skill to the ground? When

the body pales the way of sheets on which there is nothing
but white like the silent and frightened flag of surrender.

Close of ceremony nearing, and in the mirror coy between
them, jasmine-garlanded reflections leave no space

for a slip of tongue or blade, or indecent bite to split
the blanched expanse

of dread.   Bloodlust spent without blood,
blankness to explain.

Becoming Prodigal

Asphalt before us—a flat, empty Texas road
not unlike the winding voice of Hope
Sandoval on tape, singing of home.

Beside me, you sleep like the dead,
& the dusk is mine.

Fields in desert tones fade farther into blush
over limber grass, over
the metal stitching of uncoached railroad.

Milky-tipped cat-tails line mossy ponds.

Then: a sudden single burst as flame—crimson
in its tufts and bones; twining
Niconian along it's other half—the bright
invitation of serpent green.

Such a tree can only be autumnal.

Consider this: a thing beginning together,
with another,
is always bound;

its vein will fall without question back
to the same bundle of root.
However far color and branch will sway, it will
always return.

There are windmills still in Texas, nearer
than the hue of horizonpinned
hills.

& home can easily be the space between
the yellow lines on the concrete
branded into of grass.

Dismissed: the carnivals spotted over miles,
skeletal arboreta dripping Spanish moss,
lazy bovine menageries.

Instead: only the phoenix resurrection
beside so much dust. Through the distance:
this single breach of the pale.

The Truth Inside Postcards

I call her and I give her the hours of dawn to translate,
thin beams
of daylight warming the silent air in my apartment.

She masks her eyes with glasses, furrowed brows,
bustles to her bookshelf,
laying out before her lap an assortment of bound pages:
thin, too frail to carry,
fat with curling pages, scrolls like brittle
papyrus, in English, Urdu, Arabic,
and she says *Inshallah, he will make it something good;
wait, wait…
here, talk to your father while I look.*

My mother, patient oracle, tells me cryptic answers
that only my heavy heart can understand, and only
in these morning-yellow moments,
before the heavy tides of night lose the messages
hatching from swan eggs into peacock feather,
under a hurricane sky, when everything is
anticipation—*leave him if he hurts you so; you are losing
faith like the tide; there will always be words to come;
someday, you will shine like the inside of moon.*

My sisters, too, still in pajamas and last night's makeup,
will join her for tea at the table
ask her to mend their kaleidoscopic midnights into meaning
while my father fries eggs, silently listening.

Miles of telephone wire bind the dreaming—
        even as far as Omaha, gray Ohio,
        the wet-sandy monsoons in Madras—
a simple board & chain swing under a thorny, bitter-berried tree—
        the dusty, flame-colored markets of Hyderabad,
        or the dry flat horizons of Texas—
and leave my tea leaves to settle
a blurry word in my cup, a word—so much like *home.*

Leonid Shower Above 360 Overlook

i.

Crisp November hours. Still.
And the stone beneath my back is softer than sea
or river reflecting beneath.

Wide before me stretch mist and textured sky.
Quick bursts of sudden glitter, thrust
swift through cloud cover.

Night breeze thrumming a stiff chorus of leaf
sounds, muffled whispers in hidden faces.
And rock cradles arm cradles head.

Dark pulls down my eyelids, full
of the blush of the gloaming. Then silver
streams like marionette strings to keep me watching.

ii.

The *Sijjin* weighs heavy on my low left side
and I grip my right fist, to balance deed with desire.

The shades of night are slipping
over your fingertips,
        velveteen like the green whispers beside me.

No moon sickle sweet to threaten my high neck in the dark
of sky, but the crescents of nails digging into my palm will
scar like stone under ice water.

Are you counting how many per moment
little slips of falling fire?
        demons sent flailing from heaven
    with broken bits of gossip.
I measure the silent angle, the trajectory of stone.

It is only me here:

cliff face an empty plateau holding
my splayed fingers behind me,
my sprawling legs before me,
and my knees locked flat.

Doll on a bookshelf, glassy eyes dreaming
of something more real than faith,
watching the fall of heavens beneath her feet.

Kali

Under guise of autumn, she sheds
her inky scales and breeds:

Iron fingernails sculpt,
mold & assemble remnants
of iris and lip and vocal chord.

Her children move slowly
forward, hypnotic
like sea anemones under water,
with their clinical eyes fixed

on the tumble of moment after movement.

Her tendril hair she folds for them,
folds over onto a path
of trembling ground; she leads:

A fluid dance of bodied breath
as she gathers them, takes
missionary steps over old scaly flesh.

Habibi: **Beloved**

This, the *zaghreet* call in the dervish whirl
of your waist, is a shudder in the sheen of your
Dance!, now, like the serpent skinned
behind your eyes knew not how to fade.
                                          My own
eyes drinking your wavering hips. The braid
of tambourine uncoiling as you speak,
tastes like smoke, like coffee. It hangs
in my hair after you have forgotten
the scythe of crescent hanging in the slick
edge of black bladed night.
                          In you, I could
build houses, live like earthen men—made
of half spirit and half sand. Under the red
embers of coal, your lips, the swell of burning
and of exhaled smoke—Are you, behind it, only
a mirage spilling in a peasant's skirt
to appease a crowd, high waving fingers only
the cadence of rising voices, the hollow beat
of drum matching your cruel, quick feet?
                                          Nothing
but a colored swirl of light and smoke, leaved tea.

Holy Land

Inside every field of sunflowers, one
can find a field of suns—and so
every
soldier fights for something noble.
But
in each free movement by a one,
is the slavery of another. One
head held high only
because another is bowed
to give it light—a shadow anchors
every stem.
                         Nothing can exist
except in absolutes.

Every east must be another's west.

The lines we carve on maps, mortal
                  as skin.
Each split hemisphere will open
like a sliced sun.
One half falling,
held half dripping
down the grasping hand.
                              Nothing
left to balance the scale.
                              Instead,
we make fences over bones,
their gardens mark the weight of air.

Tutankhamon's Nurse

How easy—to unbury
the dead,
as if corpses might speak
over the din of epoch.

What can we do with so much
displaced sand?

At Saqqara, past mounds
of cat mummies—an
alabaster jar
of organs: a sign
that the labyrinthine tombs
waited so many suns
under sand
to give us a story—
in the heart, Maya.

You pull husks of men out
of their waiting for rebirth,
excavate
subterranean cities and
they plunder tombs
for black market gold,
sacrifice handlain
walls for the same.
Would you break the bricks
of the living to honor
your footsteps the spirit
of the dead?

Make the tallest dunes,
abandon them to sunburnt wind!

The nature of sand varies. Soft
as sun-ashes where we tread, it is
cold, dark, wet above the mummies.

We create no *shabti,*
vessels to testify our deeds,
no graven deities to protect us.
Because our deaths are
solitary.
We move
the tongues of sand
until they grant us tales
of an opulence
that we could not even want.

American Flag as *Pardah*

Baghdad, of its magic carpets, lost
one thread and another—like a crumpling row
of soldiers—in turn the rectangles folding
back over themselves and the tasseled fringes
of sky and soil met, across the horizon.

A hem was pulled from the vertical center—
one row of stitching, square knots
of windows and curtains—and another
above, higher, above, unraveling
into the collapsing spine of the building,
sides falling into the center, into a plume
like an ash flower, an asphodel—
the ghost of bodied breath swelling
under a snapping sky.

In Texas, I folded my *jah namaaz*, fringe to fringe,
to place my peace on an American shelf
beside the TV screen
on which the whistles of bursting rocket lulled
unfinished screams—
until I stopped folding
my scarf into smaller angles in my frozen hands—
my scarf on my hands, under my eyes opening,
fell open unfolding—openmouthed, unsilenced.

Blue Girl

She faces me, pearl as a blade's handle on that carpet, softer, thicker than my tongue—and it is the inside of my tongueless mouth where she stands.

Her parlor blooms with chaise lounges in black velvet & when she smokes, the cigarillo waits at the end of a wand, far from the cloud snaking through her nose. Ghosts, here, writhe, one on another on the contours, braiding each through each.

When she sees that I see, she looses a wide laugh. The inside of her mouth is outside of mine, where I stand before mirror. On her tongue is a sugarcube and in it a painted postcard of a girl in braids on floorboards spread full of splinters, crackling varnish. Torn off, the window shutters hang, hinged at bottom

like the sleeves of a bodice I did not wear. Standing in a torn slip, once pink as toenails or abalone, in a lightning slap of white.

The mirror is faded. Or. An old house always tricks its newest guests. The outline of me hangs in the reflection, grown taller—something like embers at my reaching fingertip.

iii.

The heavenly heart lies between sun and moon.

—Lu Yen

The culmination of Icarus's life:

a single, defiant splash
of color & wax.

Every rising body is an enemy
of the sun.

She. Always splitting the morning
into blanched sky, admitting nothing

like a cloud for shade
even. Just

the color of molten wax:
a stain, like ambition.

Datura

Suit of tephra for the sea
lying flat against the rifts
of ocean-bed. Crests failing
over Tokyo.
Red, the lava cooling under
rain. Not blood, my love;
nothing so alive could exist
beneath these caves, where
even sea anemones will suck
the skin until it peels away—
the burn seeps in only later,
in silence, into bone.

Eleusis

She, clothed in mourning glories,
held the dust-skinned baby.
Lifeless, it shifted in her arms
with each of her movements.

And she wonders now why she
cannot breathe back life into
the infant. He replies
with silence, glazed eyes,

face tuned to her side, away.
She is gray and ashen white
and the blue of frozen tears,
speaking to me.

I do not understand her
subterranean words—
she speaks in different tongues
inside this muddy grave.

And I
care nothing for apocalyptic gestures
and wingless children,
smooth like albatross eggs.

Alone in the Cadaver Lab

Flaps pinned once per quadrant, like moth wings,
the epidermis gapes open.

Inside the slick coils of tissue, glistening residues
of promise, is congealed the thinnest red of passion.

Face covered with a sheet, plain white sanctum, so
I do not have to know

what you might have considered a good hair day,
or what color might set off the shade

of your unblinking eyes.
From here, you are a fossil in the making.

In the striations and unwanted lumps beneath
the contours, you surface—nothing

more than a puzzle. And instead of locating the vessels
leading from one organ to another,

I cannot stop wondering if your lips are blue,
if you felt the moment approaching.

Argument

After 3.5 million years of evolution,
past amoeboid cell, bony fin,
between the bony joints of the buried
fossil and the breathing flesh,

there is no room for a mistake.

It is always a matter of life and death.
And a moment is less than the blink
of dinosaur eye, more brittle
than a peacock egg.

Elephants grieve the death of one
of their pack, carrying the smooth curved
tusks over dusty miles until their calls
cease to echo in the wounded sand.

One human tooth can never bear as much
weight. It is just as impossible
to say the words behind regret as to unbury
the body sunk into its own shadow.

Hatter madder maddest,

join me
at tea. Your chair is empty, warming
in the sun. Your bougainvilleas have shriveled
on the vine and your fruit is dead.
    And it is
daisies and posies since
your flies stuck in this honey, spreading
on the table spread.
             Eggs not fit to burst
are filling my belly, skin-seams ripping
for them. Hatch me a jungle, my babies, out
of this fleshfield—I am rotting. Time yet
is left—
       for swamp to fill the glass
place of pavement,
       for foliage and mud—
       breathless.
   Iridescence isn't
wingless, legless; it began with gills.

Birthright

We are, you say, daughters of the sun.
The night is not for women, home
of wolves and men
There, the soil splits wide. Better to fill
the hours with yellow light, to wait
inside walled space
as yellow bulbs bloom, bursting open
the seeds of dark.

Escape Artist

Harry—what were you searching for?
Racing so close to the cusp of death,
always the asymptote of the moment.

More than adrenaline lined the leather
buckles of straightjackets, chilled
those water filled tanks, latched trunks.

Did you need so desperately
to prove that immortality
was in the choosing?

And one simple punch left man
naked and vulnerable, his insides
split like a melon
in the moment beneath ordinary.

Not just illusions, you gave us magic—

the neverending search for levitation,
over a glass coffin pulsing with snakes,

the impaled woman bisected by sword,
kissed back into breathing.

Years later, someone challenges your ghost:

743 feet over Hoover Dam, he is
inversely perched under a trapeze by his toes—
96 men killed in its craft, not enough a threat—
one slip declares the certainty of ends.

Series of bodies, each suspended
by a slimmer thread, tighter knot, and
no masked figure can ever spoil with
his plain truth the ecstasy of fear.

Stitches in Rib

I saw my bones laid out before me—

my bones,
carefully arranged
in place
in that wedding gown,

flesh slipping from them,
spill
of memory like candle wax
and powder
and poppy-red mouth, glistening
a wound splitting.

Saint Teresa never lived, never
died, never felt. Neither you.

Under your words, my death shroud.

Orchard in the Texas Sun:

Peaches: orange globes bursting
the heat.
Unripened, they are not round.
But, look!
Blossoming between the leaves:
clusters of small flame.

Karkadeh

There, in a village outside Cairo—
its name I have forgotten, beginning
with a sound like
No…

Hibiscus blossoms, plump
& bright as flame wait to be plucked,
drying dark as clots of blood
in the sun.

If you have never drunk their tea red
as your open veins, tart
enough to pucker your lips unwillingly
and sweetened

with the honey of wildflowers
from the Ukraine, you have never known
the meaning of seduction, he had said—
So many kinds of crimson

falling into tastes and never
really left behind.
Watch it brew witches brew in you, water
thickening from nothing. The color

moves so slow. How long it takes to cool;
it will, always the first time, burn your tongue.

Without Freud

Inside a butterfly, a reborn soul,
said Greece.

When will I learn to cut my self open
on serrated edges?

Moth wings, *elytra, Ichneumonidae.*
Underneath, my skin.

Will I learn to love
the taste of my own blood?

iv.

The moon has set and the Pleiades
it's midnight
the hours go by.

—Sappho

Girl Friend: *Saheli*

Your *dupattah* is trailing behind
you, in the breeze like a ribbon that has
wound up and spun you, pulling your
scarf—ribboned like a snake or a bird,
green and parroting the wind. And now
you are gathering your long tunic,
khameez to cover your modesty just so,
the way of Waterhouse's Boreas or
shying Eve—just one of my sighs has
caught there, too, in the hem of your
lap.

Oh, I can catch the wind

in my skirts
like apples?

A breath,
strong enough to fill

all of my lap…

In Urdu, the wind is called
Hava, which is also how
you say Eve.

Ophelia's Ghost

You will never know
what it is to need touch
like air,
& so
I step here, toes
slipping easily

into cold, shivers
growing into sparks in my skin.

Suspended here—like swaying reeds—
every pore of my skin—
cradled;
currents at once liquid
& electric.

I curl my toes into soil;
it pools
around my ankles, my arrowhead feet.

Rooted.

Everything silk-close without the
distance of air;
rock against water against
flower against clay;
warm
slippery weeds
coil around my legs.

I raise my arms,
& twisting,
loose a mermaid scream.

St. Agnes Eve

The hem of her long white dress raking
the soil, leaves not footprints
but a path behind her, on which to arrive,
here at the seam of air and earth, water
and the fire in her anklets, under which
the splinters of the bridge slice
into her bare feet.
A cautious backward glance as she climbs
onto the edge, with
closed eyes and a deep breath.
One foot glides over the railing,
hesitates.
She comforts the ring on her finger before
easing it off.
Her eyelids coyly rise—
echoed by the corners of her lips.
Toes curled around the railing to steady
her forward leaning body, she watches
the ring ripple the surface,
her scattered image.
She descends,
adjusting the veil over her eyes,
gathers up her skirt in both hands
above the knees.
A saltless backward glance. And then
the sound of her laughter, her running feet.
Tonight she will dye her dress black.

Your Way of Apology

One for sorrow, you said.
But there was comfort in its blue sheen,
in its shroud of midnight-colored
feathers in the sun.

I stretched a bony hand to draw it nearer,
thinking only of your scarecrow gait
and bruise-soft lips;

thinking not of the thorns in the dead
bush at my side until
the gash glared angry from my arm.

And for that the raven came,
pecking not unkindly at the glistening,
syrupy wound. My arm,

drawn back, in the armor of clasped fingers.
Before me, its head cocked sideways, standing
in the small pool of sunset tears:

I saw you

again, behind the hungry mouth and eyes
searching the dead
spaces in my ribcage.

One from sorrow, I thought you said, from
across the lonely miles
in the feather-blue of night.

Dryad Unsung

Bone-dry iris cannot hold a drop
too far past thirst
                    old, cracking
when the trees are eyelashes
wrought of iron.

All the fae are dead,
                    their wings
draped limp on twigs
like leftover skins.

Corpses, though,
                    hold magic, too,
once devoured.

Port Lavaca, Texas

My sister and I walk along the curving pier.
Beside us, through slate-grey cloud cover
fat bands of sun fall down to flooded grass
where the waves ripple like melted silver.

We are looking for marsh birds.

But there are no great egrets stretching their long rope necks,
no pelicans filling cupped beaks with fish—
except in bold black strokes on the signs.

There are only Laughing Gulls
gathering in formation
like fleets of aeroplanes or small winged soldiers,
behind us.
And a series of black skimmers, lining the guardrail
beside us
that take flight one by one as we pass.
A silent fanfare of feather and beak announces our turn
of the curve to the gazebo.

Totems of summer flings carved into splintered benches, in fading
marker, M ♥ Q 4-ever, Jenni + Mark = luv, palimpsest others.
We speak of our lost loves like birds, hastening into cloudless sky;
the planks full of broken pairs
and so we empty our pockets of perfect seashells in offering:
maybe one set of carved letters will remain undefeated.

Nothing through the rows of telescopes but wave and grass,
our magnified friends splashing waves farther down the shore.

Retreating, we toss bits of Oreo and the fleet of aeroplane gulls lifts
simultaneously, some swooping to catch chocolate in orange beaks,
the rest poised mid-air and waiting.

Past the edge of pier, the waves crash at our ankles,
at a jellyfish on sea foam, caught

at the barrier between tide and dry shore.
But on the walk back, when the tide rises high,
having carried our sandals into the current, leaving us
to watch after them,
a sudden red heron hunches over, carries off its prey in sharp beak.
We stand gazing after the heron,
sandals forgotten though the sand cakes between our wet toes.

It is like this, love—predatory and perched,
ready to take flight without warning.

Muse

    for Anaïs Nin

I am in love with a dead woman
& every night, I creep in through
eyes cooled like lava under rain
& curl up fetus-style in her cold skull.

I knead the brittle bones,
as if they could be made unfrozen,
feed them with my breath. They
devour my voice, grow more brittle still.

When I emerge again,
I move—slow,
delirious and wistful,
like I am made of water.

My feet touch down as fallen eyes
drop, shatter with each step & leave
the icicle sound of blue glass,
laughter hanging the fog behind shadows.

Cairo Palace Café—Houston, TX

Walking into a well-lit hookah bar after midnight, we didn't
expect a half-empty table full of family-friends—

It was supposed to be a night for siblings, for catching up
with sisters for *I'm finally wearing lipstick again.*

In dragon-breathing moments, surrounded by exhaled apple,
grape, strawberry flavored tobacco,

it is easy to slip into the oldest shoes, into voices spoken
against the bubbling of *argila*, into stormwhile stories.

It is easy to pass these violet hours here, among the nameless
faces with the same color skin, almost-familiar accents.

So we sit here, wrapped up in smoking rows of speaking,
chess moves and carom, belly dancers, keyrkadil and mint tea.

In the center of an unexpected gathering, it feels not unlike
huddling together in a long-ago windowless room

instead of evacuating, while Hurricane Alicia's screeching
winds brought a fence down on our strawberry patches,

gifted our front lawn with an additional rooftop. Our parents'
stories of older generations fell then in the same accents

around us, songs turned to rain so hard it echoes still
in water bubbles, the sky dissipating like smoke.

To learn patience,

is to catch a scream mid-mouth.

It is like the sudden scorching sun
interrupting my night—
bat wings breaking into moths,
howl into raging siren:
ambulance wailing, 2am.

In the emergency room, much later:
Dawn—an ill fitting elegy to the moon
crescent plume faded now.
Such moments know no release,
some moments cannot be erased, reversed.

I have no mood
for a cartographer's mind, this moment

though I'm driving through
my father's groggy navigation
still sedated from his MRI—
stroke, they said—
taken this 3rd time despite
claustrophobic cold palms—
as he directs me through circuitous streets
to a Madrasi restaurant to fill a craving—
the only one he's expressed
in my twenty-four years—
for a Masala dosa.

Steering through city rush hour,
the cars around me—an Armada.

And moving slow, deliberate, I see time
ending,
realize that mortality does not wait
for the tying up of words, apologies, regrets.

Pretending he doesn't know which city we are in,
he tells me I should know the roads,
in Chicago, is it? *No, Houston, Dad.* Impatience
until I face him in the rearview mirror, grinning
in mischievous sopor.
How can I suppress a copy?
Winking at my mother's worry,
*Is that the Sears Tower? It looks shorter
from here,* I play along.

Lakeshore Boulevard: Chicago by Night

Red beam spilling from the lighthouse
across colored city lights and waves
rumple like mercury, memory on water.
Tight lip of lights from Navy Pier until
the melodrama of skyline. Before Both,
a rim of black horizon, broken,
intermittently, circuitously, by the lighthouse.
Handmade cliffs are monuments to the sun
rising out of the sediment weighing down tide.
So much silence balanced on the cusp of shore:
bright lanterns of noise, and cowering beside,
a simple statement of the sky at night
and its seabound brother, held by a thread
of rippled water speaking through seam.
Crimson Candy-Apple Red Blood Cell.

Nag's Head, North Carolina

Between the choir of waves,
voices fall onto wet sand
from shipwrecks
a hundred years ago.

It is said that pirates hung here
sheets from the thinnest trees;
billowing, they became ships—
shorelength, they strode
with the impaled
heads of wild horses held high
in focus of distant sight—
too near the vessels scouting ahead
for land.

In turning course, they crumbled
against the low jutting stone—

Mermaids' teeth,
the sea's own angry grasp:
the chicanery of pirates luring sailors
into unsung ambush.

Bursting into sea-salt, they sank,
emptied
of cargo, the animation of bones.

Horizon of ghosts walled around this
island, Nag's Head. Standing before
horses, the sea, and God,
I am left to listen: wordless
song calling from beneath the unspent tide.

V.

It was a glorious bright day, I remember, fifty by the heliometer, but already the sun was sinking down into the…down among the dead.

—Samuel Beckett, *Endgame.*

Flowers for the Dead

Her voice decaying, like butterfly wings hovers around the dark-clad figure. Black gown of laced layers and veiled face, she drifts on shadow on the bridge, holding a basket of red, red poppies. She scatters them onto the river, like salt or stillburning ash.

Once, I surfaced to a shower of blood, gathering nepenthic petals.

Her voice breeds storm clouds, a stillness in the air, crouched and waiting to pounce. Now, even the skin of the living is grayed, silent shades unweaving paths. Calling,

Flores. Flores para los muertos.

The poppy red glare against moods and the river-vein pulse, its mournful cryptic whispers. We stop to listen against the muertos, the dead that chase us.

I see her sometimes.

Wraith girl at the banks, gathering the dripping petals into her skirt, watching the crinolinecage voice waver above her. Is she wrapped in spider-webs or the beginnings of a cocoon? Bursting through her paling skin: wings, red and silver against her dark hair.

Atlas Beetle. Lily petal. Cattleheart.

Ariadne's Dream

Night—swallow me into your garden
of corpses,
shroud my living
skeleton,
whisper like this, yes, like this
against my gooseflesh with your slippery
tongue.

I can shed my old skins & weave,
serpentine
among these stones—soft to my bare feet—
before I fall
to knees kneading new soil,
exposed & luminescent
in the moon—
diamonds melting over my cheekbones.

Night—I understood faith & left it
with the empty,
gown sprawled at the bone gate.

Vandalized at the Graveyard Edge, Seraph

Dry notes seep from bone flutes,
filled with the hollow that should
have been marrow.

And as she stands here at the edge
stones fall from her mouth, shatter
on the rough concrete.

The stones like moss against the flesh
of her bare feet, moonlight slick against
shoulder and silvery hair.

So much peace in this sleepyard. Beside her
a blackened angel in sharp falling water,
watcher of the restless souls that congregate

in mourning garb, with nothing more to grieve
than Autumn. Restless, they sometimes drink
from this water, desperate to be whole.

She thinks the stone speaks to her, says it
was not some child's prank that turned the pale
stone dark. She considers this her home to guard.

Gingerbread Girl

She could cut seams down her skin, thin
as red wires they might sting. Peeling
one and then another down, bright petals
drooping
        to blanche the bones. Later,
stitch the edges up again, rag doll hems.
This crosshatched cicatrix a reminder
of unraveling, unreveling,
                        of luminescence
on a rocky moonless terrain, where
unshining pebbles cannot lead back again
to the lost way, anything like home.

Changeling in the Fire

Jungle of bones
& skin
fleshfields sinking
underfoot
moss hair hanging
low & wild.

Sing, flutes of ivory,
of the beginning, not
apart from the end.

In darkness, the heart
was won, one
of another fruit was undone,
in hunger.

Gate of bone, ribcage,
sternum,
vertebrae unclasp
& nowhere skinned,
locking
close & unopen.

Heliophobia

You were made of eggshells
        your skin smooth, cold
        heliophobic
& fragile like flowers of dust.
Your eyes shifted & congealed
        like quicksilver
& I saw myself inside them:
    unmoored, drifting.
I used to kiss your shadow so
I would not crack the surface.
Then, I thought that if I broke you
the mercury would spill out,
settle around my form.
So I held you closer,
                tighter,
until you shattered.
There was nothing
left but crumbs of shell
        like so much chipped paint
        or slivered porcelain
& your frozen eyes,
    with my likeness inside—
    all fading, jellied colors,
that had ceased shifting.

Sleeping Beauty
   after Miranda Sex Garden

When we have sex, I lie stiff
beneath you. Ribcage unstirring,
arms limp. It's easy to breathe
without moving at all. Still, there
is sometimes too much color in
my skin, too much warmth in
my body, for your taste. The labor
of hours is never too thin when
your eyes flame up—finally some
move has cracked the shell and
life spasms in reluctant song.
Persephone stolen, Leda relenting
in the instant where life is reborn. Next
time, a glass coffin might do just as well.

Shadows for Emily

You must wear your black
with a difference—
not classic—turtleneck and linen,
not clerical—habit worn,

but defiantly. Beads of jagged glass
are obsidian on your wrists. Buckles
on witch-heeled shoes. Outline the
eyes like worry.

And always keep—around your neck—
this key. Inside
its old-fashioned brass are all unlocked
doors, the smiles you hide underfoot.

Carry your shadows in your eyes,
fists—or you must live alone in them,
in shroud-white gowns
to cultivate them.

These are the balances—the dark of shade
against your silent flame.

Cat O' Nine Tails.

The cracking sound of rope-dead skin
on live skin & the buzz on the flesh,
bruises singing.

She presses face to blanket to swallow
the screams, writhes like
snakeskin shedding.

She wonders if welts scar,
salty, silent tears slipping down
to quell the skin-fires,

if it will bleed before the thousandth
lash to mark the thousand
& one nights of desired-dread

that forgot that night had a guillotine
morning after, brocade bright
& warm as melting.

She smiles up at his grimace,
knows he does not
understand

how real the stinging flesh
makes her, how
justified inside these tears.

Asylum

Under the spilling black lights
white is the moon,
and the beats of drum & step are
only the striated sounds under
cardiac skin
quickening in anticipation of
what is not—
the same four walls,
the same windowed gloom

Slick black vinyl & white
like the glare of sun,
an ambulance driver's jacket meant
for Mars.
I watch you: tall and blonde as sand—
you are everything
that I   am not.
And slipping fingers faster up one dial
there along another,
cigarette stabbed in adrenaline time—
just the close of eyelids and small
claustrophobic sway for yourself.

But there below the DJ booth,
neon is truth;
that 40 x 40 space
is not   just a littered dance floor
is   a confessional.
And if not absolving them of sin, you
have the power to steal the stab of regret.
A few hours absolution
in the womb of urban wall, in the
slick of black on black and desperation
in so much hair color
like paint in primaries.

Is it in the sway of arm or hip

that so much synthetic noise becomes
the wail of seraphim? Is it in
the glare of leather, lace, chains that
chastity can be held and innocence
lost   again, again, again?

Beating, breathing moments.
It is not about dance, or a fuck, a drug,
it is not grief:
it is only one pulsing, shivering
scream of bodies, held suspended
at the precipice without fear of slipping—far
beneath skin, for one stretch of digital dream.

Hocico

1.

Flair of vinyl blooming from his waist,
cinching there & seeping close along
torso, limb—stiff emergence from tar

A ring of spiked hair around the head,
black, too unyielding a halo, not

unlike a gutter crown.

2.

Give me a Mohawk in colors too gaudy
for mornings. I will own the night.

The Pleiades, a fanfare.
My spotlight, the moon.

Shriek of bats to protest against
the grave of night.

3.

Vocal range registering not a wail, not
a wish, only the monotony of rage.
In the scatter of bodies—disjointing
angular glides of rhythm—
a burst of supernova.

The beauty of a mosh pit is in the breaking

open—a pocket of floor space,
of memoried men, to contain
the ecstasies of doubt, to cushion
the voice too shrill to exclaim, kept
festered in the bones.

Chand Raat: Eid ul Fitr

Greensweet
henna in sugar-oil and eucalyptus,
I trace
in hair-thin coils,
along my upturned paling palms.

Beneath this
bouquet of temporary futures,
twined with blossoms opening in my night,
your own
wishes—palmlined map
to the walls of the city inside my breath.
These worldly wishes in red, drying lines—
only complements.

I go tonight,
not to the bridal chamber of a man,
but to the thinnest crescent of a moon.
Hear these, my bangles, Beloved.
Here, these my knees—cracking—
on which I kneel towards
the Easterly.

I have left it behind, Beloved.

The laughter of carnival
in the distance,
a bright-lit bazaar,
shop-keepers selling sandalwood or myrrh,
rock-sugar candy,
beads on which to count Your name.

It is enough
for me—
these knuckles: an abacus under thin skin,
a carpet of green grass blades,
the nightbirds in the wind—

and in the wind,
tendrils of my hair lifting off my nape.

Light rising from resting in contours everywhere.

ACKNOWLEDGMENTS

I'd like to thank the publications that featured earlier or other versions of some of these poems:

Arsenic Lobster: "Before the Wedding Party" and "From the Hours of Forgiveness"; *Arbor Vitae:* "First Night in the New House"; *13th Warrior Review:* "Datura"; *10x3 plus:* "Eve, Eve, and Adam...Nowhere"; *Voices of Resistance: Muslim Women on War, Faith, & Sexuality* (Seal Press, 2006): "Chand Raat: Eid ul Fitr", "Abida", "American Flag as Pardah", and "Holy Land"; *The Homestead Review:* "Becoming Prodigal"; *Diner:* "Muse"; Karamu: "heliophobia"; *Of the Divining and the Dead* (Finishing Line Press 2012, chapbook): "Chand Raat: Eid ul Fitr", "Leonid Shower Above 360 Overlook", "Lorca at the Edge of the Sea" and, "Nereid Speaking"; *TheThe Poetry Blog's Infoxicated Corner*, nominated for "Best of the Net": "Gingerbread Girl", *Limerence & Lux* (Chax Press): "Cicatrix", "Not An Apple, Only Blossoms", "Cacophony of Bells: The Origin of Disquiet", and "The Cost of Forgiving". I'd like to thank the Virginia C Middleton Fellowship, the Fania Kruger Fellowship, and the James A Michener Fellowship for supporting my work. I'd also like to express my gratitude for the love, friendship, community, support, encouragement, and inspiration that so many people in my life have given me, including: my parents Tahir & Abida Syed Razvi, Shehla Razvi and Babak Mobasheri, Suemyra Razvi and Mustafa Syed, Musa, Iliyah, Zachariah, Mubeen, Mahir, Fox Frazier Foley, Jilly Dreadful, Mary Field, Cody Todd, Neil Aitken, Josie Sigler, J Barager, Larbi Gallagher, Suraj Shankar, Jess Piazza, Kelli Anne Noftle, Amaranth Borsuk, Genevieve Kaplan, Alexis Lothian, Katy Karlin, Yetta Howard, Janalynn Bliss, Mark Marino, Matthew Siegel, Lee Ann Gallaway, Aeryck Eagle, Farid Matuk, Anna Rosen Guercio, Diana Lopez, AJ Ortega, Nikki Hutchinson Davis, Dianne Gault, Charles Alexander, Cynthia Miller, Patricia Smith, Kyle Schlesinger, Margaret Rhee, Leah Maines, Christen Kincaid, Percival Everett, TC Boyle, Mark Irwin, Dana Johnson, Aimee Bender, Eamonn Wall, Fidel Fajardo Acosta, Tom Whitbread, Judith Kroll, Naomi Shihab Nye, Khaled Mattawa, Kim Herzinger, Dagoberto Gilb, Melissa Studdard, Kimiko Hahn, Roger Sedarat, Cole Swensen, David St. John, Carol Muske Dukes, Susan McCabe, Moshe Lazar, Paul Alkon, Jeffrey Di Leo, Lauren A. Pirosko, Kauser Razvi, Raeshma Razvi, and so many more that I haven't been able name here from among my family and friends and community.

Saba Syed Razvi is the author of the Elgin Award nominated collection *In the Crocodile Gardens* (Agape Editions, 2016), as well as the chapbooks *Limerence & Lux* (Chax Press), *Of the Divining and the Dead* (Finishing Line Press), and *Beside the Muezzin's Call & Beyond the Harem's Veil* (Finishing Line Press). Her poems have appeared in journals such as *The Offending Adam, Diner, TheTHE Poetry Blog's Infoxicated Corner, The Homestead Review, NonBinary Review, 10×3 plus, 13th Warrior Review, The Arbor Vitae Review,* and *Arsenic Lobster,* and others, as well as in anthologies such as *Carrying the Branch: Poets in Search of Peace* (forthcoming), *Voices of Resistance: Muslim Women on War Faith and Sexuality, The Loudest Voice Anthology, The Liddell Book of Poetry, Political Punch: Contemporary Poems on the Politics of Identity, The Rhysling Anthology, Dreamspinning,* and *Machine Dreams.* Her poems have been nominated for the Elgin Award, the Bettering American Poetry Awards, The Best of the Net Award, the Rhysling Award, and have received a 2015 Independent Best American Poetry Award. She is currently an Assistant Professor of English and Creative Writing at the University of Houston in Victoria, TX, where in addition to working on scholarly research on interfaces between science and contemporary poetry, she is researching Sufi poetry in translation, and writing new poems and fiction.

www.ingramcontent.com/pod-product-compliance
Lightning Source LLC
Chambersburg PA
CBHW021154090426
42740CB00008B/1085